Explore Space!

Space Suits

by Deborah A. Shearer

Consultant:
James Gerard
Aerospace Education Specialist
NASA Aerospace Education Services Program

Bridgestone Books
an imprint of Capstone Press
Mankato, Minnesota

Bridgestone Books are published by Capstone Press
151 Good Counsel Drive, P.O. Box 669, Mankato, Minnesota 56002
http://www.capstone-press.com

Library of Congress Cataloging-in-Publication Data
Shearer, Deborah A.
    Space suits / by Deborah A. Shearer.
        p. cm.—(Explore space!)
    Includes bibliographical references and index.
    Summary: Describes the different types of space suits astronauts wear while on board
the space shuttle or on a space walk.
    ISBN 0-7368-1144-3
    1. Space suits—Juvenile literature. [1. Space suits.] I. Title. II. Series.
TL1550 .S5 2002
629.47'72—dc21   2001003555

Editorial Credits
Tom Adamson, editor; Karen Risch, product planning editor; Steve Christensen,
    cover designer; Linda Clavel, production designer and illustrator; Katy Kudela,
    photo researcher

Photo Credits
© Digital Vision, cover, 10
NASA, 4, 6, 8, 12, 14, 16, 18, 20

1 2 3 4 5 6 07 06 05 04 03 02

Table of Contents

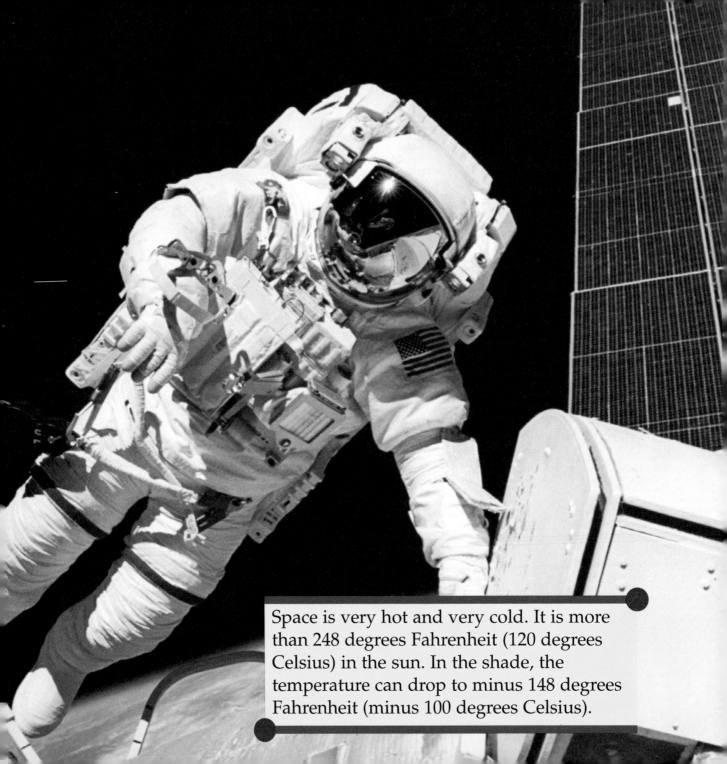

Space is very hot and very cold. It is more than 248 degrees Fahrenheit (120 degrees Celsius) in the sun. In the shade, the temperature can drop to minus 148 degrees Fahrenheit (minus 100 degrees Celsius).

Space Suits

Astronauts wear different types of clothing to work in space. What they wear depends on what they are doing. Space suits are protective clothing that astronauts wear in space. Space suits make it possible to survive in space.

astronaut

a person who is trained to live and work in space

The bright orange suits that astronauts wear for liftoff and landing often are called Pumpkin Suits. Can you see why?

Suits for Liftoff and Landing

Astronauts wear launch and reentry suits during liftoff and landing. These orange suits have a parachute and life raft. The crew may have to jump out of the shuttle in an emergency. The suits can support an astronaut for 24 hours in the water.

parachute
a large piece of strong, lightweight cloth; parachutes allow people to jump from aircraft and land safely on the ground.

Hook and loop fasteners on astronauts' pants help keep objects from floating away.

On the Spacecraft

Astronauts wear comfortable clothes on the spacecraft. They wear cotton shirts, pants, and socks. Astronauts float in the spacecraft, so they do not need shoes. The clothes include pockets for storing pens, notebooks, sunglasses, and scissors.

oxygen
tanks

Suits for Space Walks

For space walks, an astronaut wears an Extravehicular Mobility Unit (EMU). The EMU is like a small spacecraft for one person. It provides temperature controls and oxygen to breathe. Many layers of cloth and rubber make up the EMU.

space walk
a period of activity spent outside a spacecraft by an astronaut

The Helmet

Astronauts wear a helmet for launch, reentry, and for space walks. They wear a cloth cap inside the helmet. The cap has built-in microphones and earphones. Astronauts talk to each other during space walks. Outside the helmet is a visor.

visor
a shield on the front of a helmet; a visor protects astronauts' eyes from the Sun's bright glare.

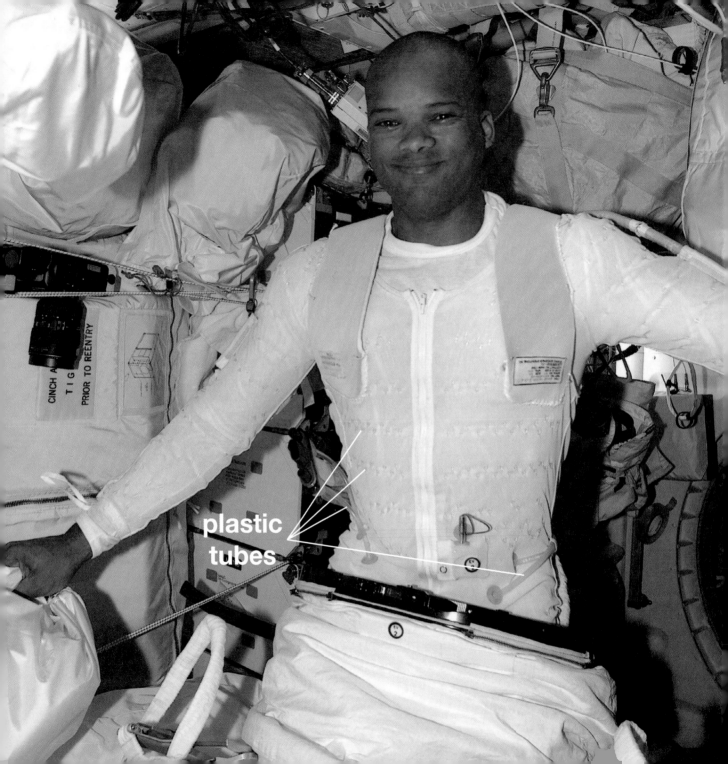

plastic
tubes

Inside the EMU

Astronauts wear a cooling and ventilation garment inside the EMU. This one-piece suit looks like long underwear. It has more than 300 feet (90 meters) of plastic tubes. Water runs through the tubes to keep the astronaut cool.

ventilation
a system that allows the flow of fresh air

Astronauts can eat during a space walk. A food bar is attached to the inside of the HUT. The food bars are made of pressed fruit, grain, and nuts. The wrappers are made from rice. The astronauts eat the wrappers too.

The HUT

Almost all other parts of the EMU are attached to the Hard Upper Torso (HUT). This hard shell protects the astronauts from space micrometeoroids. Astronauts need help to climb into the HUT.

micrometeoroid
a tiny, fast-moving space rock

The First Space Suits

Space suits have changed over time.
Early space suits were very stiff.
Astronauts could not move easily.
Scientists are working on space suits that
allow astronauts to move more freely.

This NASA painting shows what astronauts might look like as they explore Mars.

Space Suits for the Future

Astronauts will need better space suits to travel farther and stay longer in space. NASA is working on a new suit that will allow more movement. It will allow astronauts to work more comfortably on the Moon and Mars.

NASA

National Aeronautics and Space Administration; this agency is in charge of all U.S. space missions.

Hands On: The Liquid Cooling Garment

This activity will help you understand how the cooling and ventilation garment works.

<u>What You Need</u>
Large plastic trash bag
2 buckets or large pots
Ice
Water
About 10 feet (3 meters) of aquarium tubing

<u>What You Do</u>
1. Wrap your arm in the trash bag and exercise for a few minutes.
2. Take the bag off. The plastic is similar to the EMU. Was your arm hotter in the bag? Would you feel comfortable if you left it on for a long time?
3. Place one bucket on a table and fill it with ice water. Place the other bucket on the floor.
4. Wrap the tubing around your arm.
5. Put one end of the tubing in the ice water.
6. Suck on the other end until the water comes out.
7. Put this end into the other bucket on the floor.
8. How does your arm feel? Is your body beginning to cool down?

The liquid cooling garment has thousands of water tubes. The water cools the astronauts as they work.

Words to Know

emergency (e-MUR-juhn-see)—a sudden danger

extravehicular (EK-struh-vee-HIK-yuh-lur)—outside the spacecraft

garment (GAR-muhnt)—a piece of clothing

launch (LAWNCH)—to send a rocket into space

liftoff (LIFT-off)—the movement of a spacecraft as it rises off the ground

oxygen (OK-suh-juhn)—a colorless gas that people need to breathe

torso (TOR-soh)—the part of the body between the neck and waist, not including the arms

ventilation (ven-tuh-LAY-shuhn)—a system that allows the flow of fresh air

Read More

Hayden, Kate. *Astronaut: Living in Space.* New York: DK, 2000.
Walker, Niki. *The Life of an Astronaut.* Eye on the Universe. St. Catharines, Ont.: Crabtree, 2001.

Internet Sites

Johnson Space Center—Astronauts
http://www.jsc.nasa.gov/pao/public/astronauts.html
NASA Human SpaceFlight
http://spaceflight.nasa.gov
The Space Place
http://spaceplace.jpl.nasa.gov/spacepl.htm

Index